THE TAO OF ONLINESS

The Tao of Onliness:

An *I Ching* Cosmology

THE AWAKENING YEARS

MARTIN TREON

FITHIAN PRESS · SANTA BARBARA · 1989

Design and typography by Jim Cook

LIBRARY OF CONGRESS CATALOGING-IN-PUBLICATION DATA
Treon, Martin, 1937–
    The Tao of onliness: an I Ching cosmology—the awakening years /
Martin Treon.
        p. c.m.
    ISBN 0-931832-25-X : :$8.95
        1. Cosmology—Miscellanea.   2. Consciousness—Miscellanea.
3. I. ching—Miscellanea.   4. Tao—Miscellanea.   I. Title.
BD701.T69   1989
299'51442—dc19   89-31086 CIP

Published by Fithian Press
P.O. Box 1525, Santa Barbara, CA 93102

The Tao of Onliness:

An I Ching Cosmology
The Awakening Years

Prologue
(9)

"When the great tao is gone, 'humanity' and 'equity' appear. When 'intellect' and 'education' emerge, the great fakes will appear. When the six relations do not harmonize, 'filiality' and 'affection' will appear. When the state breaks up or breaks down, the 'statesmen' and 'patriots' will appear.

"Heaven is not 'humane,' and Earth is not 'humane.' They take the ten thousand things as dogs of straw. The sage is not 'humane.' He takes the hundred clans as dogs of straw."

—Lao Tsu
from *The Taoist Vision*

Prologue

"And at the moment of enlightenment he (Dogen-zenji) exclaimed, 'There is no body and no mind!' When he said 'no body and no mind,' all his being in that moment became a flashing into the vast phenomenal world, a flashing which included everything, which covered everything, and which had immense quality in it; all the phenomenal world was included within it, an absolute independent existence. That was his enlightenment."

—Shunryu Suzuki
from *Zen Mind, Beginner's Mind*

In what follows, the space-time reality frame of reference is of course the necessary medium in description and discourse of the learned one's Isantis Tao cosmology in the context of his Awakening. However, Isantis Tao cosmology itself is not significantly concerned with this space-time reality consciousness. Rather, it is the description of a vision of the unfathomable totality of transcendent Consciousness, the transfinite mystery of Tao Incarnate, here called Isantis Tao.

Although infinitely complex and varied within itself, space-time reality spectrum is here viewed as but one peripheral and insignificant consciousness reality among the infinite realities of transcendent Consciousness. In turn, focal human consciousness within space-time reality, what Merrell-Wolff calls "egoistic" or "world field" plane of temporal human consciousness, plays an exceedingly infinitesimal and insignificant role within the totality of space-time consciousness reality.

In this cosmology there is simply *no* manifestation, realization, expression, or "thing" at all, no matter how apparently mundane or inconsequential, which Realized in Its transcendent completeness is not an absolute Face of the *whole* of Consciousness Itself. Thus is such inherent Realization everywhere and always with each individual human consciousness; this innate immediate Face of all that Is andor Is-not andor is Neither . . . , here called transcendent Consciousness, which is Isantis Tao. Indeed, this One Mind of individual human consciousness Realizing Itself, even in the most apparently trivial and unimportant daily life detail, *is* absolute Transfiguration and Awakening. And it is the particular texture and course of one such individual Awakening that is described in what follows.

■

" 'What are we really doing, don Juan?' I asked. 'Is it possible that warriors are only preparing themselves for death?'

" 'No way,' he said, gently patting my shoulder. 'Warriors prepare themselves to be aware, and full awareness comes to them only when there is no more self-importance left in them. Only when they are nothing do they become everything.' "

—Don Juan
from *The Fire from Within*

CHAPTER ONE

The Face of Reflexivity

"It is too clear and so it is hard to see.
A dunce once searched for fire with a lighted
 lantern.
Had he known what fire was,
He could have cooked his rice much sooner."
 —Mu-mon from *The Gateless Gate*
 from *Zen Flesh, Zen Bones*

"**O**nly the dancing shadow of the smoke from my pipe on the stream that *is*, remains."

The learned one is astounded to hear the ragged mute seated next to him speak so. Or speak at all for that matter. For this vagabond had not spoken a word in the years the learned one had known him. Indeed, he was generally considered to be both mad and mute. A penniless and homeless psychotic person.

The learned one, out of compassion for his plight, had befriended the mute. And not infrequently they would sit together, as now they did, on this bank by the stream within view of the lake. The learned one had come to enjoy the quiet warmth and solace that the mute's presence somehow brought.

It is a warm and dry Autumn afternoon. Indian Summer. The two sit together on the grass and dry leaves by the stream. The sun is behind them.

Learned one (Lo): Your words are profound, but I am dumb-founded at hearing them from you. I implore you to speak on.

The mute looks upon the stream.

Lo: Please go on! What do you mean by these words? Will you not elaborate?

Silence.

Lo: I wonder, did you really speak at all or was it my imagination? If you did, I beg you to speak on . . . Will you not further clarify your meaning?

Silence.

Lo: When I consider the sequence of enlightenment of the *10 Bulls* of Zen, I feel myself to be at the third level. That is, "Perceiving the Bull":

"I hear the song of the nightingale.
The sun is warm, the wind is mild,
willows are green along the shore,
Here no bull can hide!
What artist can draw that massive head,
those majestic horns?" (Reps, 1957)

while you are at the tenth level, "In the World":

"Barefooted and naked of breast,
I mingle with the people of the world.
My clothes are ragged and dust-laden,
and I am ever blissful.
I use no magic to extend my life;
Now, before me, the dead trees become alive."
(Reps, 1957)

Unmoved, the mute smokes his pipe and looks upon the stream.

Lo: With conception I divide my heart. Yet it consumes me also, illuminating both far and near. I envy you! You are balanced and well grounded, and I am not. While you are centered, I am top-heavy. Knowing that language conception divides meaning, presents only the illusion of meaning, still I persist in this expressive mode. What a profound fool!

The mute, without expression, turns his head and looks upon the learned one. Gradually his gaze returns to the stream, and then his face turns from the learned one completely and toward the distant lake.

Lo: Of the three gunas, my heart is divided between Sattwa and Rajas (Swami Prabhavananda and Isherwood, 1951). But even beyond my longing for knowledge binding me on the one hand, and my passion for pleasure and possession binding me on the other, is my attachment to language conception itself. Certainly creativity lies beyond such attachment. This hawk (pointing skyward) is not attached to the image of flight, lest it would fall to the ground.

The mute now looks upon the stream.

Lo: Though its flight is premature, and though apart from air and sky it does not wing, still I pursue this illuminative conception. And when it strikes the ground and breaks its wing, I mend it. Thus is its flight and the way of its accord. And in this way is its beauty apparent and its power hidden from view.

The mute, smoking his pipe, remains in his muse.

Lo: Let me gather wood-blocks from the pile to illustrate the form and relation of this cosmology.

The learned one walks to the woodpile and returns with an armload of assorted blocks of finished lumber four-by-fours, two-by-eights, two-by-fours, and two-by-twos. Once again seating himself beside the mute, he recites a twelve-hundred year old Taoist saying:

Lo: "Wild geese fly across the sky.
    Their image is reflected on the water.
    The geese do not mean to cast their image on the water.
    The water has no mind to hold the image of the geese."

Silence.

Lo: The foundation of my cosmology *Is*. Its source is of the Watercourse Way. Its namelessness is rooted in the Tao (Watts, 1975).

He places two foot-long two-by-eights next to one another on the ground between himself and the mute.

Lo: The foundational *flow* of this cosmology, its wellspring, is the process of polarity-within-unity. The relational principle of Yin and Yang. Its foundational *form* is (pointing to the first block) the Transexistential reality of Yang, and (pointing to the second block) the Existential reality of Yin. The Transexistential reality (pointing to the first block): How is the inconceivable conceived? It is that which we are, which we are not. Indeed, It is as Genesis 1:2 suggests, darkness-upon-the-face-of-the-deep. It is that which is most profoundly transparent. For Christ It is The Holy Spirit.

The learned one fleetingly looks to the mute for some response, but there is none.

Lo: The Existential reality (pointing to the second block): How is the conceivable conceived? It is that which is, which we are. Indeed, It is as Genesis 1:2 suggests, the Spirit-of-God-moving-upon-the-face-of-the-waters. It is that which is most profoundly apparent. For Christ It is the process of the Father and the Son.

The learned one places two foot-long four-by-fours on the Existential two-by-eight.

Lo: The fundamental form of Existence is (pointing to the first four-by-four) the Yang reality of the flow of unreflexive *experience* symbolized through this vertical line and *I Ching* solid-line hexagram (which he draws in the dirt with his finger) (Figure 1). And (pointing to the second four-by-four), the Yin reality of the flow of reflexive *awareness* symbolized through this crossing horizontal line and *I Ching* broken-line hexagram (which he draws in the dirt) (Figure 1). This hexagram (pointing to the six solid lines' hexagram) called "The Creative Principle"

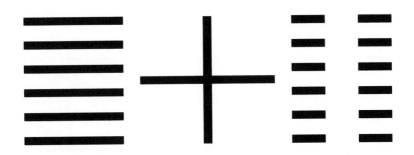

FIGURE 1.

symbolizes the creative power and righteousness, the sublime virtue, of the celestial forces of change (Blofeld, 1968). This hexagram (pointing to the six broken lines' hexagram) called "The Passive Principle" symbolizes the all-embracing power and tranquility, the sublime softness and silence, of the receptive terrestrial forces (Blofeld, 1968). Thus, unreflexive experience and reflexive awareness are the two *fundamental* polar realities of this *first* and deepest dimension of Existential reality symbolized in this image (Figure 1).

Silence.

Lo: The power of *experiential* reality transfigures all Existence. Of this transfigurative flow is created all configuration. This is the *creative* reality of void. In Genesis it is "the light Day; the firmament Heaven." For Christ it is God the Father. J.C. Pearce (1975) calls this Primary Processing. The *power* of infinite and open reality synthesis.

The mute belches audibly just as the last word is being spoken. The learned one is momentarily distracted.

Lo: The vision of the reality of *awareness* configures all Existence. Through this configurative flow is the manifestation of all transfiguration realized. This is the *productive*

15

reality of form. In Genesis it is "the darkness Night; the dry *land* Earth and the waters Seas." It is Christ Himself. J.C. Pearce (1975) calls this Reversibility Thinking. The *vision* of infinite and open reality synthesis.

The learned one breathes deeply now. He turns to look at the mute who continues to look upon the stream. Without turning his head, the mute strikes a match and rekindles his pipe.

Lo: (reciting from the *New Testament*):

"Master, we know that thou art true, and teachest the way of God in truth, neither carest thou for any *man*; for thou regardest not the person of men.

"Tell us therefore, What thinkest thou? Is it lawful to give tribute unto Caesar, or not?

"But Jesus perceived their wickedness, and said, Why tempt ye me, *ye* hypocrites?

"Shew me the tribute money. And they brought unto him a penny.

"And he said unto them, Whose *is* this image and superscription?

"They said unto him, Caesar's. Then saith he unto them, Render therefore unto Caesar the things which are Caesar's; and unto God the things that are God's."

In this way Christ reminds us to carefully distinguish between superficial aspects of the apparent reality of *reflexive* awareness, in this instance the personal temporal reality of image and superscription, and the fullness of the transparent reality of *unreflexive* experience; the reality of God the Father.

Silence.

Lo: Thus is the Holy Trinity of this conception of Being (pointing to the first four-by-four); the Father, who is the creative power of transfigurative experience; the Son (pointing to the second four-by-four), who is the productive vision of configurative awareness; and (pointing to the first two-by-eight), the fathomless Transexistential reality of The Holy Spirit.

The mute's apparent response is audible flatulence. Again, the learned one is distracted and slightly surprised at the timeliness of the mute's apparent retort. He glances at the mute whose eyes are closed and head is leaning slightly forward. He appears to be napping yet his pipe is in his hand and smoke is rising from it. The learned one erases the first symbol in the dirt (Figure 1) and replaces it with another of similar design (Figure 2). It is late afternoon and there is a warm dry breeze.

Lo: This (pointing to the diagram in the dirt) is the symbol of the *second* ring of Existential reality (Figure 2). Within it are contained the four cardinal mode realities of Existence. The two lesser cardinal modes of *compassion*, which is represented by the right horizontal projection of this segmented cross (pointing) and hexagram thirteen called "lovers, beloved, friends, like-minded persons, universal brotherhood" (Blofeld, 1968), and *knowledge*, represented by the left horizontal projection of this cross (pointing) and hexagram sixty-four called "before completion" (Blofeld, 1968). And the two greater cardinal modes of *communion*, represented by this upper vertical projection and hexagram eleven called "peace" symbolizing heaven and earth in communion (Blofeld, 1968), and *meaning*, represented by this lower vertical projection and hexagram eight called "unity, coordination" (Blofeld, 1968).

The learned one places a foot-long two-by-four on its face midway between and on top of the four-by-fours so as to cover the crack between them (Figure 3). He then places two four-inch long two-by-twos on the middle one-third of each four-by-four, adjoining the two-by-four. Thus is formed a cross design resting on top of the four-by-fours (Figure 3).

Taking a pencil from his pocket, the learned one carefully draws the Yin-Yang line patterns of the two *greater* Hsiangs ($\equiv$ and $\equiv\equiv$) and the two *lesser* Hsiangs ($\equiv\!\equiv$ and $\equiv\!\equiv$); the four Hsiangs of the *I Ching* (Legge, 1964; Blofeld, 1968), one Hsiang pattern on each extension of the cross. Finally, next to

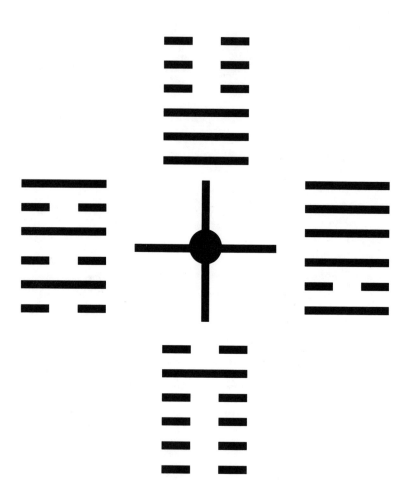

FIGURE 2.

each Hsiang he draws its two component trigrams (Legge, 1964; Blofeld, 1968) (Figure 3).

Lo: The vertical dimension of this wood-block cross (pointing to the apparent vertical projection marked with the two greater Hsiangs $\equiv\equiv$ and $=$ $=$) symbolize the *greater cardinal polarity* of communion and meaning. Communion ($\equiv$) arises from experiential reality, and meaning ($=$ $=$) from awareness. The horizontal dimension of this cross (pointing to the apparent horizontal projection marked with the two lesser Hsiangs $=$ $=$ and $=$ $=$) symbolize the *lesser cardinal polarity* of compassion and knowledge. Compassion ($=$ $=$) arises from experiential reality, and knowledge ($=$ $=$) from awareness.

Silence.

Lo: Of the *I Ching*'s four Hsiangs (pointing respectively to the four projections of the wood-block cross of Figure 3, and quoting from William Blake):

"The eyes of fire ($=$ $=$),
the nostrils of air ($=$ $=$),
the mouth of water ($\equiv$),
the beard of earth ($=$ $=$)." (Erdman, 1976)

i am *action* of fire $\equiv\equiv$ and thunder $\equiv$ $\equiv$ called
   compassion
i am *intuition* of wind $\equiv\equiv$ and water $\equiv$ $\equiv$ called
   knowledge
i am *power* of lake $\equiv\equiv$ and Heaven $\equiv$ called
   communion
i am *vision* of earth $\equiv$ $\equiv$ and $\equiv$ $\equiv$ mountain called
   meaning

compassion: i am transforming *energy* of fire
knowledge: i am conforming *consciousness* of wind
communion: i am transfiguring *bliss* of lake
meaning: i am configuring *confluence* of earth

compassion: i am thunder, *inspired* by Brahman
knowledge: i am water, *comprehending* through Brahman

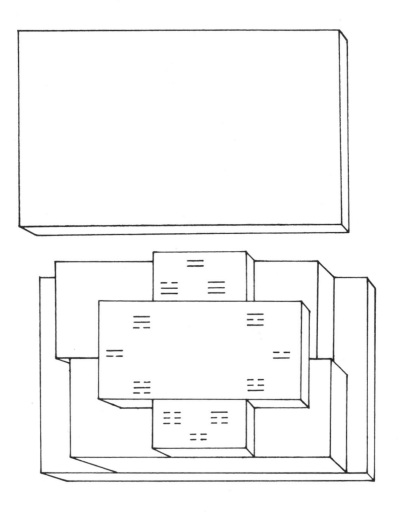

Figure 3

communion: i am Heaven, *infused* with Brahman
meaning: i am mountain, *realized* in Brahman

compassion: incomparable is my brilliance and strength,
    even the mountain is moved
knowledge: incomparable is my firmness and acceptance,
    even the earth is eclipsed
communion: incomparable is my strength and loss, even
    the mountain vanishes
meaning: incomparable is my repose and acceptance
    even the earth is encompassed

compassion: i am summer, the form of experience
knowledge: i am winter, the void of awareness
communion: i am spring, the void of experience
meaning: i am autumn, the form of awareness

of astrology's four triplicities (Oken, 1973):
compassion: i am aries-leo-sagittarius, the fiery force of
    spirit
knowledge: i am gemini-libra-aquarius, the airy element
    of mind
communion: i am cancer-scorpio-pisces, the watery ele-
    ment of soul
meaning: i am taurus-virgo-capricorn, the earthy force of
    form

compassion: i am resonance of grace, touching *each each-
    where*
knowledge: i am truth of essence, understanding *all all-
    where*
communion: i am unity of source, being *one all-where*
meaning: i am genesis of root, seeing *none each-where*

compassion: i am daylight of southern skies
knowledge: i am night of northern skies
communion: i am auroral skies of east
meaning: i am twilight of western skies

compassion: i am *presence*, none dare stand with me
knowledge: i am *stillness*, none dare stand before me
communion: i am *transparency*, none dare stand beyond
    me
meaning: i am *vortex*, none dare stand above me

compassion: i am now-here, *passion* of worlds
knowledge: i am perfect fullness, *cognition* of worlds
communion: i am perfect emptiness, *creation* of worlds
meaning: i am nowhere, *conception* of worlds

compassion: i am *attention*, illumination of worlds
knowledge: i am *perception*, silence of worlds
communion: i am *dispersion*, awakening of worlds
meaning: i am *cohesion*, implosion of worlds

compassion: i am *intensity* of sun
knowledge: i am *psyche* of moon
communion: i am *potency* of sky
meaning: i am *fertility* of earth

The learned one now selects a four-inch length of two-by-
four, and on its face from corner to corner draws two intersect-
ing lines. He places this two-by-four face up on top of the wood-
block cross design (Figure 4).
Lo: In this second ring of Existence, i am four-fold Trinity:
        i am Father, communion and meaning (pointing to the
            two greater Hsiang projections)
        i am Son, compassion and knowledge (pointing to the
            two lesser Hsiang projections)
        i am Existence, Holy Spirit (pointing to the lines' inter-
            section in Figure 4)
    Silence.
Lo: Here then is the central visage, the crux, of this second
        dimension of Existential reality. And like the realities of

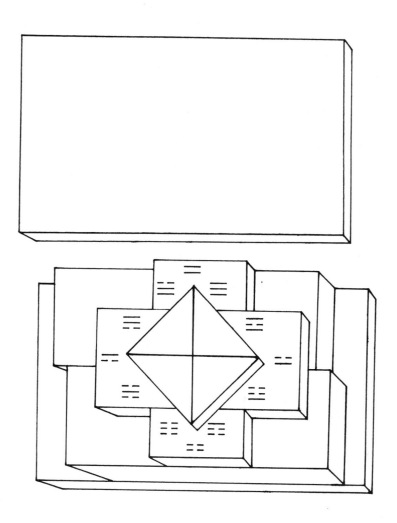

Figure 4

each dimension of Existence, these four cardinal mode realities of this second ring of Existence find only tangential realization within that consciousness which is the space-time frame of reference. The central realization of each reality at each ring of Existence is *completely* beyond this space-time reference frame.

Silence.

The mute places his pipe upon the ground. Slowly stretching his arms and torso, he yawns with a deep and booming voice. To the learned one the mute appears totally indifferent and self-contained.

Finally the mute struggles to his feet, walks to a nearby tree and proceeds to go about the process of urinating. This completed, he returns, seats himself and resumes his pipe smoking. The learned one observes all of this without comment.

Lo: I have shared with you my intuitive perception of this awesome world. Will you now share with me the further meaning and portension of the words you have spoken?

There occurs a long silence. The learned one looks upon the face of the mute. The mute looks upon the watery stream that dances by. The silence continues.

The mute suddenly turns his face to the man of learning. Without attending, the mute effortlessly strikes a match and ignites the dry grass and leaves at the base of the learned one's pile of blocks. The blocks ignite.

The learned one at once draws back and at the same time is, through his eyes, drawn to the flame. He gazes into the dancing flame and is deeply silent.

The fire's intensity increases from red to white hot. The blocks are consumed in flame. Loose leaves and twigs around the fire are drawn into it. It becomes like a blast-furnace. Gradually the earth at the base of the fire appears to melt and is drawn into the flame. And although the fire remains contained, it grows in ferocity.

The earth upon which the two men sit is melted and the men themselves melt and are drawn into the flame. Even the air and the water of the stream appear to melt and are consumed in this focused inferno. Finally, all of this reality collapses into the intense flame and is *totally* consumed.

The flame alone remains. And gradually it too dies away and is gone out. Nothing appears, except the face of reflexivity. And only the dancing image of reflexivity itself on the stream that *is not*, remains.

■

"If a fool would persist in his folly he would become wise."

—William Blake (Erdman, 1976)

CHAPTER TWO

Reflection, Shadow, and Illusion

"In this way and that I tried to save the old pail
Since the bamboo strip was weakening and about
to break
Until at last the bottom fell out
No more water in the pail!
No more moon in the water!"

—Chiyono
from *The World of Zen* (Ross, 1960)

"**O**nly the stilled reflective surface of this lake realizing itself itself, awakens from illusion. But the realizations of our awakening is yet shadow, within shadow, within shadow."
Learned one (Lo): Again you speak to me directly without directly speaking. I understand this now and no longer desire that you elaborate.

A mute person is seated beside the learned one. Without expression the mute looks upon the lake before them and smokes his pipe. The two are seated on the sandy shore of the lake into which flows the stream they had sat beside in another time. Except once in that time by the stream and again just now by the lake, the learned one had never heard the mute express himself in words.

It was out of compassion for the mute's plight that the learned one had originally befriended him. But over the years the learned one came to realize that just the opposite had actually occurred. That is, the mute, out of compassion for the learned one's dark and empty life, had become his friend and teacher.

Lo: Sage, I have learned so much from you and am so grateful to you. When I now consider the sequence of enlightenment of the *10 Bulls* of Zen, I know that I have made that quantum leap from the third level, "Perceiving the Bull," to the fourth level, "Catching the Bull":

"I seize him with a terrific struggle.
His great will and power are inexhaustible.
He charges to the high plateau far above the cloud-mist,
Or in an impenetrable ravine he stands." (Reps, 1957)

While you continue your way at the tenth level, "In the World":

"Barefooted and naked of breast,
I mingle with the people of the world.
My clothes are ragged and dust-laden,
and I am ever blissful.
I use no magic to extend my life;
Now, before me, the dead trees become alive."
(Reps, 1957)

Unmoved, the mute smokes his pipe and looks upon the lake.

Lo: Yet I am a timid and fearful man, holding tight to my cosmology like a baby to its mother's empty breast. You have somehow weaned yourself of attachment to such empty pretension; such obsessive discourse and explication. Indeed, while I attempt to escape from life through such illusion, you escape *to* life, *in* life, *through* life itself. I still envy you!

The mute, distorting his face completely out of shape and stretching his mouth open so wide that the learned one becomes alarmed, yawns in a booming voice and then, closing his eyes, lies back upon the sandy beach.

It is summer twilight and a campfire ringed with stones burns before them. Beside them is piled a small stack of firewood. Behind them sway the towering pines. The lake is quiet except for sounds of water softly lapping the sandy shore. There is a small island covered with trees perhaps half a mile from this shore and toward the middle of the lake. It is nearly dark and no moon is in the sky.

Lo: As I have said, the foundation of my cosmology *Is*. Its source is of the Watercourse Way. Its namelessness is rooted in the Tao. Indeed, so clear and fluid is the Tao that It may be arbitrarily arranged in any conceivable—or inconceivable—fashion so that the fit is perfect. Yet how is the arranger arranged but by the Tao? And who is it that presumes to arrange clarity and fluidity itself? So opaque and impenetrable is the Tao!

"The Tao that can be told is not the eternal Tao.
The name that can be named is not the eternal name.
The nameless is the beginning of heaven and earth.
The named is the mother of ten thousand things.
Ever desireless, one can see the mystery.
Ever desiring, one can see the manifestations.
These two spring from the same source but differ in name;
this appears as darkness.
Darkness within darkness.
The gate to all mystery."

—Lao Tsu from *Tao Te Ching*

The mute is quietly snoring on the sand.

Lo: The deepest meaning and broadest context of this cosmology can best be understood in this Zen story:
"Two monks were arguing about a flag. One said: 'The flag

is moving.'

The other said: 'The wind is moving.'

The sixth patriarch happened to be passing by. He told
   them:

'Not the wind, not the flag; mind is moving' "
   —Mu-Mon from *The Gateless Gate* (Reps, 1957)

The mute slowly rises to a sitting position and, rekindling his pipe, looks steadily into the fire.

Lo: In this cosmology, the foundational polarity of *Existence* and *Transexistence* ultimately arises from the Tao. It is the unfathomable Source of this polarity at Its awakening *in* and *through* and *with* and *of* the Tao, that is the Holy Trinity of Christianity, the Perfect Enlightenment of Buddhism, the righteous transcendent God of Abraham of Judaism, the singular transcendent Allah of Islam, the unified and universally shared transcendent God of Baha'i Faith, and the indwelling Atman, Brahman the Divine Ground of Being of Hinduism.

Silence.

Lo: At the deepest dimension of Existence arises the *fundamental polarity* of the two fundamental realities of *experience* and *awareness* (the learned one draws Figure 5A in the sand between himself and the mute). Arising from and returning to experience is the greater cardinal reality of *communion,* and the lesser cardinal reality of *compassion.* Likewise, arising from and returning to awareness is the greater cardinal reality of *meaning,* and the lesser cardinal reality of *knowledge.* There exists between these four cardinal realities the *greater cardinal polarity* of communion and meaning, and the *lesser cardinal polarity* of compassion and knowledge. The firelight of this deepest fundamental dimension of Existence casts but four transcendent shadows: is-is, is-are, is-am, is-not, yet only one is-seen. These are the four cardinal mode realities of the second ring of Existence: *knowledge, compassion, meaning,* and *communion* (the learned one alters Figure 5A

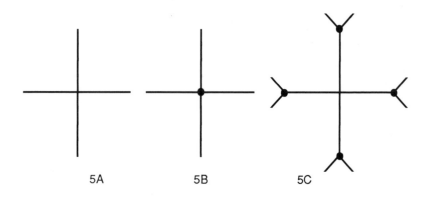

5A   5B   5C

Figure 5

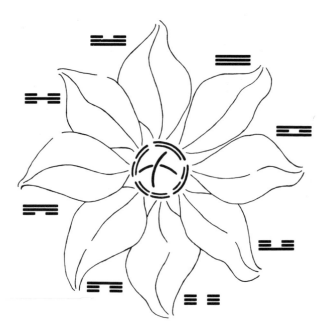

Figure 6

to form Figure 5B). The eight elemental realities of the third dimension of Existence came to me in a dream I will tell you of now (the learned one alters Figure 5B to form Figure 5C). In all, the polar aspect of this cosmology contains six concentric dimensions. These first three form the lower "trigram" as it were of this six dimensional "hexagram" of polar reality.

Without expression, the mute is audibly flatulent with perfect timing. The learned one ignores the mute's apparent "reply."

Lo: Initially in my dream there appears a moonlit flower moving in the wind (he erases Figure 5 and draws Figure 6 in the sand, but without the eight surrounding trigrams of the *I Ching*). Swaying in the moonlight, its beauty and sweet fragrance engulf me completely. And then suddenly transfixing, its satin textures reveal in reflection the relation of lines of the *I Ching* (Blofeld, 1968 and Legge, 1964). The two single lines of Yin and Yang within the bud (pointing to the image in the sand). The four double lines arising from these two which, turning upon themselves, bridge the petals and the bud (pointing). The eight triple lines arising from these four which form the petals of this fragrant flower (viewing counterclockwise, the learned one draws each of the eight trigrams of Figure 6 beside its corresponding petal as outlined and reflected in the moonlight). Merged and thus transfixed, flower, moonlight, wind, and moving mind reflect:

"When the deep mystery of one Suchness is fathomed,
All of a sudden we forget the external entanglements;
When the ten thousand things are viewed in their oneness,
We return to the origin and remain where we ever have been."

—from *Transmission of the Lamp* (Suzuki, 1960)

It is night and blackness now engulfs the two solitary figures seated in the dancing firelight.

Lo: In this dream I am seated before a campfire on a wind-swept butte in the dry and beautifully desolate badlands of western North Dakota. It is dusk and the smell of sage is in the air. In this vast sea of rugged buttes and deep ravines I am alone. Using a stick, I draw this image (he points to the flower) with its eight trigram symbols in the hard clay before me.

The joyful sage, K'an ☵ who is *clarity*, appears
in radiant beauty, K'an ☵ sits facing the fire and to my
    left
illumination's fire
this calm and righteous being
the glory of worlds!

Sun ☴ who is *through-ness*, the quiet sage, appears
steadfast, Sun ☴ sits facing the fire and to my right
pursuing no goal or destination
these serene eyes
this generous quiet presence

The holy sage Chen ☳, who is *luminosity*, appears
in tranquil beauty, Chen ☳ sits facing the joyful sage,
    across the fire
gentle and unassuming presence
this glad acceptance
concealing righteous determination

The vital sage Li ☲, who is *with-ness*, appears
fierce and dispassionate, Li ☲ sits facing the quiet sage,
    across the fire
this intensity and clarity of purpose
ice and fire!
this trusted and bounteous presence

The radiant sage K'un ☷, who is *fertility*, appears
undisturbed, K'un ☷ sits at the left side of the holy sage
inspired beauty and abundance
this radiant and regal face
a glowing warmth

The concealed sage Ken ☶, who is *in-ness*, appears
sitting between K'un ☷ and Sun ☴, Ken's parka-clad

face is hidden from view
this well of meaning's deep repose
in these cold waters each element of Existence
finds its dark reflection
   The profound sage Tui ☱, who is *unity,* appears
in deep contemplation, Tui ☱ sits facing the radiant
    sage, across the fire
holy and revered teacher
this supreme vision and acceptance
embracing all the earth
   The empty sage Ch'ien ☰, who is *of-ness,* appears
unmoved, Ch'ien ☰ sits facing the concealed sage,
    across the fire
intense and righteous persistence
this coarse enduring face
these peaceful eyes
   The nine of us sit about the fire in silence. The joyful
sage speaks:

    K'an ☵ : i am clarity
             transessence of worlds
             i am knowledge's form
             mind of joy
    Sun ☴ : i am the abandonment of conception
             peeling away identity, ideality, recognition,
               and imagination
             i am the void of knowledge
             essential emptiness
  Chen ☳ : i am the luminous vision
             receptivity and grace
             i am compassion's form
             holy embodiment of worlds
     Li ☲ : i am the thirst of fire
             iridescence of worlds!
             i am compassion's void
             the source of warmth and beauty
    K'un ☷ : i am fertility
             the root of meaning

                    i am meaning's form
                    multiplicity
Ken ☶ : i am seed of mountain
                    genesis of wind
                    i am meaning's void
                    inherency of worlds
Tui ☱ : i stand at the vantage point
                    envisioning this limitless still expanse
                    i am communion's form
                    foundation of worlds
Ch'ien ☰ : i stand in bliss and peril
                    at the threshold of the wind
                    i am communion's void
                    the soundless wind

There is silence.

K'an ☵ : i am realization of illusion
                    the formless form
                    of wheat,
                    i am the stalk and grain itself
Sun ☴ : i am fluidity
                    streaming's perfect realization
                    i am through-ness
                    intuition's heart
Chen ☳ : i am complete embrace
                    germination of all relatedness
                    of wheat,
                    i am the harvest
Li ☲ : i am love's righteousness
                    attention's perfect realization
                    i am with-ness
                    searing fire of presence
K'un ☷ : i am diversity
                    reflection's perfect realization
                    of wheat,
                    i am the seed

Ken ☶ : i am
ubiquity's perfect realization
i am in-ness
the supreme reflection

Tui ☱ : i am oneness
serenity's perfect realization
of wheat,
i am the field

Ch'ien ☰ : i am the source of transparency
perfect emptiness of worlds
i am of-ness
transparent potency of worlds

Again there is silence.

K'an ☵ : all each-where is my name
transparent Creative Principle
i am fire upon the mountain
The Traveller in view and relation

K'an ☵ draws this hexagram from the *I Ching*
in the hard dry clay:

☶
☲

Sun ☴ : all all-where is my name
transparent Creative Principle
i am mountain in the center of the earth
Modesty in view and relation

Sun ☴ draws this hexagram in the clay:

☷
☶

Chen ☳ : each all-where is my name
transparent Creative Principle
i am thunder in the center of the earth
Return in view and relation

Chen ☳ draws this hexagram in the clay:

☷
☳

Li ☲ : each each-where is my name
transparent Creative Principle
i am lightning and accompanying
     thunder
Gnawing in view and relation
Li ☲ draws this hexagram in the clay:

K'un ☷ : none each-where is my name
transparent Creative Principle
i am fire above the lake
The Estranged, Opposites in view and
     relation
K'un ☷ draws this hexagram in the clay:

Ken ☶ : one each-where is my name
transparent Creative Principle
i am land rising above the lake
Approach in view and relation
Ken ☶ draws this hexagram in the clay:

Tui ☱ : one all-where is my name
transparent Creative Principle
i am a tree growing upward from the
     earth
Ascending, Promotion in view and
     relation
Tui ☱ draws this hexagram in the clay:

Ch'ien ☰ : none all-where is my name
transparent Creative Principle
i am fire upon the wind
A Sacrificial Vessel in view and relation
Ch'ien ☰ draws this hexagram in the clay:

There is a long silence. Finally, I speak:
as water of perfect stillness is no longer itself yet knows
    itself complete
so K'an's silent mind is universe incarnate
as universe is silent mind complete

in movement is created the illusion of form
in stillness is form complete

moving in the winds of knowledge
Sun ☴ is the great voyager
standing on the highest peak

how provocative, how profound is the wind of Sun's
    awakening!
the creator and destroyer of worlds

moving in the vast currents of oceans
Chen ☳ is the singular beacon
the incandescent body of love

great is the luminous body of love!
the righteousness of worlds

the wind, at once fierce and gentle, many and one
moves over the earth and enfolds it completely
Li ☲ , enfolding the earth like the moving wind, is the
    luminous power of love

great is the source of love's awakening!
the fire of worlds

as the sea of wind ebbs and flows across the prairie
    grasses
the movement of each blade creates a world of meaning
many are K'un's faces!

great is the fire of prairie's fierce meaning!
the consummation and illumination of worlds

as the mountain's highest vision is rooted in the earth
so the light of meaning's deepest vision
is rooted in the night

great is Ken's thirst!
the wellspring of worlds

like the lake's deep dreams
Tui's complete reflection
is awakening worlds

like the giant redwood, Tui's towering visage stands
    alone
and is the beauty of worlds

like the pristine lake in which no water can be seen
the clarity of Ch'ien's presence is complete
this hidden spring, the power of clarity complete

this voyager who travels upon the wind behind the wind
Ch'ien ☰ , tempered in adversity, is come home!

K'an ☵ : of knowledge, i am the rocky sea-cliff
Sun ☴ : of knowledge, i am the expansive sea
Chen ☳ : of compassion, i am the green oasis
Li ☲ : of compassion, i am the expansive desert
K'un ☷ : of meaning, i am the mountain
Ken ☶ : of meaning, i am the expansive prairie
Tui ☱ : of communion, i am the lake
Ch'ien ☰ : of communion, i am the expansive forest

    The nine of us sit together in silence. Black night now surrounds us. The eight figures are just visible in the glowing firelight embers. As this light fades these images gradually disappear, and are finally totally engulfed in darkness. Again I am alone. And in this way ends my dream.

For a long time the learned one and mute look steadily into the fire. Suddenly the learned one turns and looks upon the mute whose arm extends upward with index finger pointing to the starless sky. The mute's expressionless face turns toward the learned one. Steady and unblinking, the mute's fierce gaze strikes a primordial terror in the heart of the learned one. A rain begins to fall on these two figures transfixed in the firelight. They are unmoved, unresponsive to the rain. The fire, smothering in the rain, begins to sputter and flicker. Progressively, darkness engulfs this scene. The two appear suspended in time, like images in marble.

The rain comes down suddenly roaring and fierce, drowning the fire. A total and consuming darkness prevails. The intensity of this darkness is as blinding in its own way as the fire of the sun is in light. The rain now ceases as suddenly as it began, and there is a moment of complete silence. It is into this intensely silent darkness that all of this reality finally collapses and is *totally* consumed, and is no more.

The darkness alone *is* and remains. And gradually it too dies away and is gone out. Nothing appears, except the face of reflexivity. And only the dancing image of reflexivity itself in the darkness that *is not*, awakens from illusion.

■

"I tell you solemnly, before Abraham ever was, I Am."

—Jesus

CHAPTER THREE

Anti-mirrors, Inversive Visions, and Savage Dreams

"Thirty spokes share the wheel's hub;
  It is the center hole that makes it useful.
  Shape clay into a vessel;
  It is the space within that makes it useful.
  Cut doors and windows for a room;
  It is the holes which make it useful.
  Therefore profit comes from what is there;
  Usefulness from what is not there."

—Lao Tsu
from *Tao Te Ching*

"**E**bony hawk (pointing skyward), high-soaring sentinel, Consciousness only—beyond even Awakening's dreams."

Looking skyward to where the mute is pointing, the learned one sees the hawk's silhouette high above them swaying in the moonlight. The learned one is pleased to hear the mute speak to him once more.

A campfire crackles and sparks before two men seated on the sandy shore of an island in the middle of a lake. It is a warm and breezy mid-summer night and the moon is full. Behind them sway the birch and towering pine. Before them waves are lapping rippled shores. A mute and a man of learning look upon the fire.

Over their years together the learned one had gradually come to resemble the mute in many ways. Both now appeared as coarse and shabby looking men. For as long as the learned one could recall, the vagabond sitting next to him had generally been considered to be both mad and mute. Yet during these years the learned one had retained some semblance of social standing. However, he too was now viewed in social disrepute as at least an eccentric if not himself quite mad. In any case, both were known and in an offhand way accepted in the social community, if primarily avoided and ignored. In fact this seemed to suit the both of them just fine.

Learned one (Lo): Yesterday while splashing water in my cup to clean it, I *was* joyous union, immediate Self complete.

The mute's expressionless face turns to the learned one. His eyes appear to survey the man of learning seated next to him.

Lo: Considering now the sequence of enlightenment of the *10 Bulls* of Zen, I am aware that I have realized the fifth level, "Taming the Bull":

"The whip and rope are necessary,
Else he might stray off down some dusty road.
Being well trained, he becomes naturally gentle.
Then, unfettered, he obeys his master." (Reps, 1957)

Meanwhile you continue your way at the tenth level, "In the World":

"Barefooted and naked of breast,
I mingle with the people of the world.
My clothes are ragged and dust-laden,
and I am ever blissful.

I use no magic to extend my life;
Now, before me, the dead trees become alive." (Reps, 1957)

Unmoved, the mute smokes his pipe and looks upon the distant moonlit clouds beyond the lake.

Lo: I feel tired and weak. Still entangling myself in the nets of my own fragmentive schemes. Learning to run full speed at a stand-still. I see the great indifference in your eyes, yet whine for you to help me. To save me from myself! Awakened one, I still envy you.

The mute rekindles his pipe, appearing completely oblivious to the learned one's monologue.

Lo: As don Juan (Castaneda, 1981) so rightly puts it, all of our endeavors are expressions of human folly, and it becomes the task of the warrior to contain his or her folly. And indeed, to contain my folly has been my central theme and core concern in this cosmology's formulation. Yet I know that in my attachment to formulation *itself,* to conception *alone,* are planted the seeds of this cosmology's inauthenticity. Thus attached, I build the foundation of its subsequent trivialization with my own hands. Still clinging—even to my own mortality. Still a profound fool!

As usual, the mute is resoundingly flatulent with perfect timing. The learned one pretends to ignore him. For awhile the learned one is silent and looks into the fire.

Lo: I call this cosmology Isantis Tao. It is a perennial conception. Of vision and metaphor, of harmony and wholeness, of nature and awakening. Nothing new and original, just old and original. Like a mountain stream that's flowing to the sea.

The mute lies back upon the beach and stretches his body in the sand. He closes his eyes and appears to be falling asleep.

Lo: This transpersonal conception is rooted in meditation, personal humility and simplicity, supreme joy, and ultimately non-attachment and non-action. Of non-action, Lao Tsu expresses it well:

"In the pursuit of learning, every day something is acquired.
In the pursuit of Tao, every day something is dropped.
Less and less is done
Until non-action is achieved.
When nothing is done, nothing is left undone.
The world is ruled by letting things take their course.
It cannot be ruled by interfering."

(Feng and English, 1972)

Lo: Of non-attachment to action, which is an expression of non-action, Krishna speaks to the warrior Arjuna in the "Yoga of Renunciation" of the *Bhagavad-Gita* (Prabhavananda and Isherwood, 1951) and says:

"United with Brahman,
Cut free from the fruit of the act,
A man finds peace
In the work of the spirit.
Without Brahman,
Man is a prisoner,
Enslaved by action,
Dragged onward by desire.

Happy is the dweller
In the city of nine gates (the human body)
Whose discrimination
Has cut him free from his act:
He is not involved in action,
He does not involve others.

Do not say:
'God gave us this delusion.'
You dream you are the doer,
You dream that action is done,
You dream that action bears fruit.
It is your ignorance,
It is the world's delusion
That gives you these dreams."

Lo: Finally, the Zen story called "The Moon Cannot be Stolen"

(Reps, 1957) brilliantly illuminates non-attachment's essence:

> "Ryokan, a Zen master, lived the simplest kind of life in a little hut at the foot of the mountain. One evening a thief visited the hut only to discover there was nothing in it to steal.
>
> Ryokan returned and caught him. 'You may have come a long way to visit me,' he told the prowler, 'and you should not return empty-handed. Please take my clothes as a gift.'
>
> The thief was bewildered. He took the clothes and slunk away.
>
> Ryokan sat naked, watching the moon. 'Poor fellow,' he mused, 'I wish I could give him this beautiful moon.' "

The mute is quietly snoring, asleep on the sand. For a long while the learned one looks out upon the windswept waves dancing in the moonlight.

Finally, the mute awakens and slowly rises to a sitting position. From this position he reaches over to the pile of wood nearby and places two logs upon the fire. Sparks fly as the fire cracks and spits.

Lo: Now, for a final time, I mend the wing
of this illuminative Onliness conception.
For this last time enabling its flight
and the way of its accord.
As I have said,
the source of this cosmology is of the Watercourse Way.
Its namelessness is rooted in the Tao.
And while it is true
that the foundation of this cosmology *Is*,
it is also true that the foundation of *Is, Is-not.*
I call *Is-not*
the Absolute Void of Infinite Consciousness.
Here named Isantis Tao.
Supreme Holo-gnostic Unity.
Unfathomable transfinite Mystery.

Not the eternal Tao, but Tao Incarnate.
Buddhism's "Pure Light of Void."
Hinduism's indwelling Atman; Brahman. Divine Ground
    of Being.
The singular and transcendent Godhead
of Judaism, Christianity, Islam, and Baha'i Faith.

  Isantis Tao
  Sacred One
  Far side of the moon.

  Isantis Tao
  Righteous One
  Only, Only, Only.

  Isantis Tao
  Transcending One
  Unfathomable Core.

  Isantis Tao
  Universive One
  Being and Nonbeing.

  I Am
  Isantis Tao
  Far side of the moon.

Without expression, the mute looks upon the dancing flames. The learned one continues:

  Emerging from and returning to Isantis Tao
  is the Supreme Polarity of *Being* and *Nonbeing*.
  Being's process is versive polarity-within-unity.
  Nonbeing's process is inversive unity-within-polarity.
  The *perfect movement* of Being's *flexive* consciousness.
  The *perfect stillness* of Nonbeing's *anti-flexive*
    consciousness.
  Being is the realization of *transcendent Holostructure*.
  Being's foundational realization
  at the wellspring of form and flow in this cosmology
  is emergence of the polarity-within-unity

of the two foundational realities of Being:
Existence and *Transexistence.*
Being's fundamental realization
at the deepest dimension of Existential reality
is emergence of the polarity-within-unity
of the two fundamental realities of Existence:
experience and *awareness.*
Being's cardinal realization
of the second ring of Existential reality
is emergence of the polarity-within-unity
of the four cardinal mode realities of Existence:
communion, meaning, compassion, and *knowledge.*
Finally, Being's elemental realization
of the third ring of Existential reality
is emergence of the polarity-within-unity
of the eight elemental realities of Existence
the features of which are
of-ness, unity, in-ness, fertility,
with-ness, luminosity, through-ness, and clarity,
and the cores of which are:
transparency, serenity, inherency, multiplicity,
righteousness, holiness, intuition, and *realization.*
   The mute rekindles his pipe.
Lo: World-honored One, over our years together
     I have described to you only this *versive* realm of Being.
     Only the infinite *form* and *flow* of polarity-within-unity
     of Isantis Tao cosmology.
     Let me now make fertile this conception,
     let it be useful and whole,
     through description of its *transcendent Holo-energy.*
     That awesome *inversive* realm
     of Nonbeing's perfectly stilling
     anti-flexive consciousness.
     The infinite *void* and *stillness* of unity-within-polarity.

     Nonbeing None
     Infinite Void

Pervasive One
Nowhere seeking You
Will I be found.

Empty None
Luminous Void
Hidden One
Creative Anti-mirror
Of dark inversive dreams.

The mute clears his phlegm-filled throat with a ghastly gutteral rasp. Summoning up the phlegm, he hurls it into the hissing fire with a pop-like spitting sound. The learned one smiles broadly to himself.

Lo: In Isantis Tao cosmology
    Nonbeing's only realization,
    the two faces of Its "form and flow" in Being,
    is the foundational polarity-within-unity
    of *Istence* and *Antistence*.
    Nonbeing's void, *Antistence*
    in polarity with Being's form, *Existence*.
    Nonbeing's form, *Istence*
    in polarity with Being's void *Transexistence*.
    Four Eternal polarities:
    Existence-Transexistence, Istence-Antistence,
    Antistence-Existence, and Istence-Transexistence.
    Four Universive realms:
    Antistence, Nonbeing's primal void
    Existence, Being's universal form
    Istence, universal form of Nonbeing's primal void
    Transexistence, primal void of Being's universal form.
    William Blake's words from "The Four Zoas" express this
        well:
  "And these again surrounded by
      four Wonders of the Almighty,
  Incomprehensible, pervading all,
      amidst and round about;
  Fourfold, each in the other reflected:

they are all named Life's—in Eternity—
Four Starry Universes going forward
    from Eternity to Eternity." (Black's Readers Service,
        1953)
Lo: Antistence is that which is-not,
    of which we cannot comprehend.
    Istence is that which is-not,
    of which we can comprehend.
    Existence is that which is,
    of which we can comprehend.
    Transexistence is that which is,
    of which we cannot comprehend.

The mute smokes his pipe and appears to be looking at the moon. With his finger the learned one draws the Taoist Yin-Yang image (Figure 7) in the sand between himself and the mute. Reaching over to the edge of the ring of stones which contain the campfire, he gathers the warm dark ashes there and sprinkles them over the sand to form the dark areas of this configuration.

FIGURE 7

Lo: Of this ancient symbol of the process of Yin and Yang
      (pointing):
    Yang is *Antistence* (pointing to the large light area),
    Yin within Yang is *Istence* (pointing to the small dark
       area),
    Yin is *Existence* (pointing to the large dark area),
    and Yang within Yin is *Transexistence* (pointing to the
       small light area).
  Silence.

Lo: Though it has taken many years, my description to you of
    the genesis and elemental nature of Isantis Tao cosmol-
    ogy is now complete. This prelude of Holistent concep-
    tion. This prologue to savage dreams.

The learned one turns to the mute. The mute looks steadily
into the flame. Finally, the mute gets to his feet and walks to a
nearby birch tree. Kicking with his tattered boot, he creates a
depression in the earth near the base of the tree. Lowering his
bib overalls, he squats and proceeds to defecate into the
depression. Meanwhile he braces himself holding onto a
branch of the tree. As usual the mute proceeds slowly and with
deliberation. He strips leaves from the birch with his free hand
and carefully cleans himself, dropping these into the depression. This completed, he hooks his overalls, pushes earth back
into the depression and packs it down. The mute returns to
the campfire and sits down. The learned one watches all of this
with great amusement.

There occurs a silence during which both men look upon
the flame. Breaking this stillness, the mute picks up his pipe
and with a twig cleans its cooled ashes into his hand. He raises
his arm and scatters these ashes so that the breeze carries
them into the fire. The fire's luminosity suddenly increases,
although its heat remains the same.

The mute continues to clean his pipe and so scatter its
ashes into the flame. The fire's radiance immediately intensi-
fies so that it is nearly blinding. Progressively, light engulfs this
scene so that it appears as daylight all around these two men
seated on the shore.

Although the fire and its heat remains contained, its light continues to grow in ferocity. The two figures appear transfixed in light. This core of blinding and consuming luminosity now gradually expands to engulf and embrace these two beings. Finally, the brilliance of this expanding radiance completely consumes and so embraces *all* of this reality, which is no more.

Light alone *is* and remains. And gradually it too dies away and is gone out. Nothing appears. Only.

■

"If the doors of perception were cleansed
every thing would appear to man as it is, infinite."
—William Blake

CHAPTER FOUR

Dead Leaves and Living Shadows Moving In the Wind

"His heart is with Brahman
His eyes in all things
Sees only Brahman
Equally present,
Knows his own Atman
In every creature,
And all creation
Within that Atman."
from *The Bhagavad-Gita*

Among the rocks and native grasses
high along the windy sea cliff
recluse woman, learned man embrace.
In awhile they sit together
at their place of meditation
overlooking windswept waters.
Isolated, silent figures
on a grassy ridge together
high above the rhythmic pounding surf.
Rocks above, around, below them

dwarfed by this majestic sea cliff
and the vastness of the ocean.

Recluse: Child of Consciousness,
              know that every thing returns
              complete unto Itself.
              Unto the Oneness of Its infinity.
              Unto the self-realizing mirror
              of Its Awakening.
              Unto Its own transparent self-abiding Am.

              Often had this island dreamer
              seeking solace and communion
              found them in this woman's presence,
              in her peerless words and actions.

              For a long while they sit silent
              ragged recluse, learned drifter,
              warm and sunny tropic morning,
              both looking northward to the sea.

Learned one (Lo): Sage, I am become Consciousness alone.
                        That which I was and ever Am to be.

A long silence falls between them.

Lo: Once more I dreamed resplendently last night.
       Dreamed of flowers moving in the wind
       radiant in auroral skies of dawn,
       seen through transcendent Existential eyes.

Lo: A vision of the Way of Watercourse
       whose namelessness is rooted in the Tao.

       Unfolding paper from his pocket
       the learned one spreads it before them.

Lo: Isantis Tao is beyond transcendence.

This total Incarnation of the Tao.
Faceless Face of unfathomable Tao.
Radiant Void of Onliness Itself.

Lo: Isantis Tao and Consciousness are One.
      And nothing Is save Consciousness Itself.
      Nothing Is-not save Consciousness Itself.
      Not Is and not Is-not save Consciousness.
      And on, and on, and on, and on, and on . . .
      Sage, This is *One none Onliness alone.*

Lo: This first of the four visions of my dream (pointing to
          Figure 8).
      Infinitely ringed holomorphic view
      of Consciousness in Existential form.
      One of the Faces of Isantis Tao
      from Its vast infinity of Faces.
      Six inner rings of polar Consciousness (pointing),
      these six rings of polar Isantis Tao.
      This outer ring and its infinity (pointing)
      of concentric prime-numbered clustered rings (pointing)
      symbolize transpolar Transconsciousness.
      These rings of transpolar Isantis Tao.

Lo: This is the *Absolute Polarity,*
      this Polarity *of* polarity,
      between what I call polar Consciousness,
      which is *Holistential* reality,
      and that called transpolar Transconsciousness,
      which is *Transholistent* reality.

Lo: Sage, emerging from and returning to
      polar Isantis Tao reality
      are the two Supreme transcendent Faces,
      the Face of Being and of Nonbeing.
      All that is transpolar Transconsciousness
      likewise emerges from and returns to
      the realm of *transpolar Isantis Tao.*

Figure 8.

Two Absolute Faces of Consciousness
which are at one in Consciousness Itself.
Two Foundational Waves of Consciousness
in actless waters of transfinite One.
Thus peerless Foundational Trinity:
that of Isantis Tao or Consciousness,
transpolar, and polar Isantis Tao.

Silence not engulfs these figures
as they view the shimmering sea.

Lo: Metaphor is the essential *substance*
of this Isantis Tao cosmology.
This view is unpossessed of *literal*
conceptual pattern, design, or scheme.
Devoid of literal form and meaning.
Possessed of universal metaphor.
Filled with figurative form and content.
Infinite allegoric odyssey
of Illuminated Awakening.
Sage, not a vision of the journey's Way,
rather, merely one way of journeying.
It is but one single snowflake image
among patterned snowflake infinities.
Its meaning found not in what is spoken
but in essence what remains unspoken.

Now the woman's eyes are heavy
as she lies back on the grasses.
Soon she sleeps in tropic splendor.
The learned one enjoys her beauty
sensing now her female presence.
Long are they like this together
before the woman's eyes are opened
and soon she sits upright again.
He unfolds another paper
spreading it on ground before them.

Lo: World-honored One, from these inner rings
    (pointing to the six inner rings of Figure 8)
    emerge the second vision of my dream.
    This second holomorphic diagram (pointing to Figure 9).
    Transcendent *polar Consciousness* alone
    viewed in this Existential form complete.
    Six concentric Yin-Yang ring relations.
    Polar Isantis Tao's six dimensions
    of which I spoke so very long ago.
    Here symbolized in *six line* hexagrams
    (pointing to the outer ring)
    of the ancient *I Ching* or Book of Change.
    In the *six points* of the Star of David too.

Lo: This inner trigram's *Existential* rings
    (pointing to the three inner rings).
    However, it is these three outer rings (pointing),
    this outer trigram, which concerns my dream.

Lo: Recall, the two lines of this inner ring
    (pointing to the singular Yin – – and Yang —— lines)
    symbolize the *two fundamental* realms
    of polar Existence reality.
    First *Existential fundamental* ring.

Lo: And these four double lines of Yin and Yang (pointing)
    here symbolize the *four cardinal* realms
    of polar Existence reality.
    Second *Existential cardinal* ring.

Lo: And these eight triple lines of Yin and Yang (pointing)
    symbolize the *eight elemental* realms
    of polar Existence reality.
    Third *Existential elemental* ring.

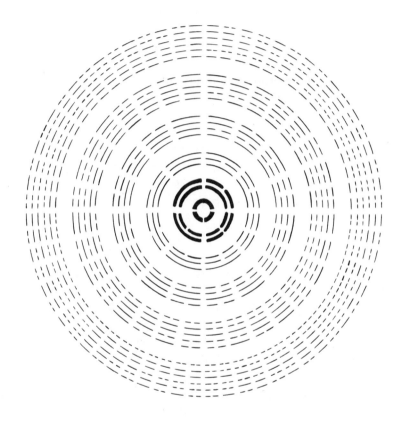

Figure 9.

Lo: In this dream-vision I did darkly glimpse
      converging of the Tao of Onliness
      with essence of the *I Ching* hexagrams,
      and saw the meaning of Wholeness Itself.

      The recluse woman calm and silent
      looking on the sunswept ocean
      finally turns to view the dreamer
      and to look upon the paper
      laying on the ground before them.
      The learned one looks closely at her
      but her face gives no expression,
      and then as quickly as no warning
      the dreamer's side she pinches sharply.
      The learned one looks stunned, then puzzled.
      Soon both are laughing with each other,
      and slowly silence rests between them.

Lo: This outer trigram's Holistential rings
      (pointing to the three outer rings of Figure 9).
      Rings *of* and *beyond* Existential realm.

Lo: Sage, this fourth ring's quadruple Yin-Yang lines
          (pointing),
      comprising sixteen polar quadrigrams,
      symbolize the *sixteen absolute realms*
      and the *eight absolute polarities*
      of Holistential polar Consciousness.
      This is *Absolute* polar Consciousness.
      First *Holistential fundamental* ring.

Lo: This fifth ring's pentad lines of Yin and Yang (pointing),
      forming thirty-two polar pentagrams,
      symbolize the *thirty-two supreme realms*
      and the *sixteen supreme polarities*
      of Holistent Being and Nonbeing
      which is *Supreme Polarity* Itself.

58

I call this *Supreme* polar Consciousness.
Second *Holistential cardinal* ring.

Lo: Birthless realms of Being and Nonbeing
(gesturing to the thirty-two pentagrams).
Realities of Being's boundless *Bliss,*
and realms of Nonbeing's boundless *Freedom.*
These realms of Being's *holomorphosis,*
and of Nonbeing's *hologenesis.*
Being's *manifestive* realities,
the profound *mystery* of Nonbeing.
The unspeakable *grandeur* of Being,
the transcendent *suchness* of Nonbeing.
Being's sublime and numinous *Beauty,*
the transfinite *Wonder* of Nonbeing.
The infinite ocean of Being's *Form,*
the anti-ocean *Void* of Nonbeing.
Realities of Being's *consciousness,*
realms of Nonbeing's *anti-consciousness.*
Each by the Other founded and sustained,
Each within Other seeded and contained.

Lo: This sixth ring's *I Ching* hexad Yin-Yang lines
(gesturing to the sixty-four *I Ching* hexagrams
of Figure 9),
forming sixty-four polar hexagrams,
express *sixty-four universive realms,*
thirty-two eternal polarities,
of Holistent *Istence* and *Antistence*
and of *Existence* and *Transexistence.*
These *four Universive realities,*
and their *four Eternal polarities.*
This *Universive* polar Consciousness.
Third *Holistential elemental* ring.

In the distance sounds of thunder
yet here the sky is nearly cloudless.
High above the gulls are crying,

below the rhythmic waves are crashing.
The sea absorbs the quiet woman
whose face remains without expression.
The learned one now looks upon her
and also is absorbed in silence.

Finally taking the first image (Figure 8)
he puts it on the flat rock near them.
Using black crayon from his pocket
he draws three figures on the white rock
and under each he writes a word.

Lo: Sage, this is the third vision of my dream (Figure 10),
comparing the four Universive realms
(gesturing to the four-sectored image on the rock)
as seen through eyes of Existential form.
This is Existence and this Antistence (pointing to each
     in turn).
Here is Istence, and here Transexistence.
Four serene Eternal polarities
emerge from and return to these Four realms:
polarity of Istence-Antistence,
and that of Existence-Transexistence,
Existence-Antistence polarity,
and finally Istence-Transexistence
(pointing to these pairs in turn).

Lo: Revealing in contrastive metaphor
each Universive realm's *reality*.
Showing the relational character
of each of the four Universive realms
and their four Eternal polarities.

For a moment there is silence
which is broken by the recluse
with a resonant resounding belch.
Smiling to himself, he pauses
then he turns his head to see her.
She is smiling Cheshire-cat-like.

ANTISTENCE ISTENCE

TRANSEXISTENCE EXISTENCE

Figure 10.

He begins to laugh and shortly
both lie sprawling on the grasses
laughing at and with each other.
Gradually they both grow silent
lying on the grass together
watching gulls and clouds a-floating.

In awhile they sit in stillness
at their place of meditation
silent as the stones about them.
Finally he unfolds a paper
and spreads a diagram before them
writing one word at each trigram (Figure 11).

Lo: This is the final vision of my dream (pointing to Figure
       11).
     Two flowers gently moving in the wind.
     Two-flowered view of polar Consciousness,
     again as seen through Existential eyes.
     Two Holistent Universive flowers,
     and fusing here upon a common stem (pointing).
     Two flowers dancing on a gentle breeze
     in glowing faint auroral skies of dawn.

Lo: As in my dream of many years ago,
     these two blooms become suddenly transfixed.
     Now revealing satin textured outlines
     describing *I Ching* lines of Yin and Yang.

Lo: In the line and outline of each petal
     is one of the eight trigrams of *I Ching*
     arranged in Fu Hsi opposition way (Blofeld, 1968)
     (pointing in turn to these four polar oppositions).
     This is the structure of polarity
     inherent in the six-ringed diagram's (Figure 9)
     outer trigram's opposition pattern.
     In this trigram of Holistential realm.

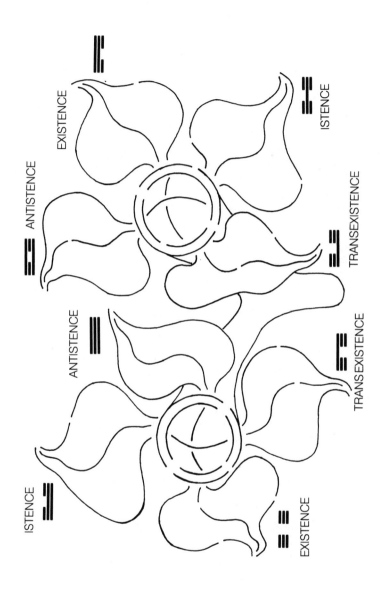

Figure 11.

Lo: This single common stem symbolizes (pointing)
the unity, source, and destination
of that called the Supreme Polarity
of transcendent Being and Nonbeing
within what I call polar Consciousness.

Lo: The lefthand flower's stem symbolizes
the unity, source, destination of
two *greater* Eternal polarities
within Supreme Polarity Itself.
Each one *between* Being and Nonbeing;
between Pan- and Trans- gnostic realms as well.

Lo: The righthand flower's stem symbolizes
the unity, source, destination of
two *lesser* Eternal polarities
again *within* Supreme Polarity.
And of these two lesser polarities,
one is within Being's reality
between that called Being's Pan-gnostic realm
and Being's Trans-gnostic reality.
The other is within Nonbeing's realm,
between Pan-gnostica of Nonbeing
and that called Nonbeing's Trans-gnostic realm.

Lo: The two buds' central Yin-Yang images (pointing),
the polar unigrams of Yin and Yang,
symbolize the singular polar Face (– – ——)
of that called the Supreme Polarity
of transcendent Being (– –) and Nonbeing (——).

Lo: The two polar digrams of Yin and Yang
of the left flower's circular border (pointing)
which act to bridge this bloom's bud and petals
symbolize the singular polar Face (= = ==):
the *greater* Eternal polarities.
Thus these two Eternal polarities,
each one *between* Being (= =) and Nonbeing (==);
between Pan- and Trans-gnostic realms as well.

Lo: The two polar digrams of Yin and Yang
   of the right flower's circular border (pointing)
   bridging the bud and petals of this bloom
   symbolize the singular polar Face (⚎ ⚏):
   the *lesser* Eternal polarities.
   Thus these two Eternal polarities,
   one in Being and one in Nonbeing,
   between Pan-gnostic (⚎) and Trans-gnostic (⚏)
      realms.

Lo: Now viewing in a clockwise direction
   so as to view from bottom line to top,
   the left flower's four petals' lines reflect
   four of the eight trigrams of the *I Ching.*
   The four Universive realms of this bloom.

Lo: The two polar trigrams of Yin and Yang
   which comprise this bloom's vertical petals
   symbolize the singular polar Face (☰ ☳):
   the *greater* Eternal polarity
   between Nonbeing's Pan-gnostic *Istence* (☰)
   and Being's Trans-gnostic *Transexistence* (☳).

Lo: The two polar trigrams of this left bloom
   which form its two horizontal petals
   symbolize the singular polar Face (☷ ☷ ☰):
   the *greater* Eternal polarity
   between Being's Pan-gnostic *Existence* (☷ ☷)
   and Nonbeing's Trans-gnostic *Antistence* (☰).

Lo: Viewing in a counterclockwise manner
   so as to view from bottom line to top
   the right flower's four petals' lines reflect
   the remaining four trigrams of *I Ching.*
   The four Universive realms of this bloom.

Lo: The two polar trigrams of this flower
comprising the two vertical petals
symbolize the singular polar Face (☳ ☶):
the *lesser* Eternal polarity
between Nonbeing's Pan-gnostic *Istence* (☳)
and Nonbeing's Trans-gnostic *Antistence* (☶).

Lo: This bloom's remaining two polar trigrams
which form its two horizontal petals
symbolize the singular polar Face (☰ ☱):
the *lesser* Eternal polarity
between Being's Pan-gnostic *Existence* (☰)
and Being's Trans-gnostic *Transexistence* (☱).

Lo: Thus, these four Eternal polarities,
of which two are lesser and two greater,
of four Universive realities.
This vision of the flowers of my dream.
Fragrant Holistent Universive blooms.

Lo: Once more the two flowers begin to move,
dancing once again in morning breezes.
Gradually they fade into whiteness
and in this way ends my two-flowered dream.

The recluse one in peaceful slumber
rests upon the native grasses
while the learned one in silence
looking out upon vast waters
rests in deepest meditation.

Thus do they remain together
for a long while deep in silence.
Finally the recluse wakens
and seating herself by the dreamer
the two gaze on the sea together.

Suddenly, and without effort,
the woman gathers all three papers
there upon the grass before them.
Rising up, the recluse holds these
walking to the windy cliff ledge
she releases these three drawings
to the gusting winds about her.
Each floats out and swirls above her
gliding high round one another
tossing like the waves below them.

Recluse: Vagabond dreamer,
        yours are the shadows
        of distant dreams,
        the glow of dying embers.
        Shadow dancer,
        (pointing to the wind borne papers)
        these are dead leaves
        and living shadows
        moving in the wind.

As the recluse ceases speaking
the floating papers flare and burn.
The fires spread to form one fire,
the flame's intensity increases
growing now from red to white hot.

Gazing into this inferno
the learned one is stunned in wonder
and profoundly deep in silence.
Although the blaze remains contained
its ferocity increases
melting everything around it,
drawing all into its vortex.
The sky itself and the ocean
appear to melt and are consumed.
The rocky sea cliff, man and woman

melt into flame and disappear.
This entire reality
collapses into the inferno
and is now *totally* consumed.

The flame alone is and remains.
Then slowly it too dies away
and thus Nothing appears. Only.
Gradually Apparency
Its very Self becomes Transparent
and Nothingness too "disappears."
Alone, Transparency transpears.
Transparent Onliness "remains."

∎

"One thought fills immensity."
—*William Blake*

"One time, Chuang-tzu dreamed he was a butterfly, flitting around, enjoying what butterflies enjoy. The butterfly did not know that it was Chuang-tzu. Then Chuang-tzu started, and woke up, and he was Chuang-tzu again. And he began to wonder, whether he was Chuang-tzu who had dreamed he was a butterfly, or was a butterfly dreaming that he was Chuang-tzu."

—Chuang-tzu
from *The Taoist Vision*

References

Black's Readers Service. (1953). *The Works of William Blake: Selected Poetry and Prose*. Roslyn, NY: Black's Readers Service by special arrangement with Random House, Inc.

Blofeld, J. (translator and editor) (1968). *I Ching: The Book of Change*. New York: E.P. Dutton & Co., Inc.

Castaneda, C. (1981). *The Eagle's Gift*. New York: Pocket Books, Simon & Schuster, Inc.

Castaneda, C. (1984). *The Fire from Within*. New York: Simon & Schuster, Inc.

Erdman, D. (1976). *The Selected Poetry of William Blake*. New York: New American Library, Inc.

Feng, G., and English, J. (1982). *Tao Te Ching*. New York: Vintage Books.

King James Version: *Holy Bible*. New York: World Publishing Co.

Legge, J. (translator) (1964). *I Ching: Book of Changes*. New York: Bantam Books, Inc.

McNaughton, W. (translator) (1971). *The Taoist Vision*. Ann Arbor, MI: University of Michigan Press.

Merrell-Wolff, F. (1973). *Pathways Through To Space: A Personal Record of Transformation in Consciousness*. New York: Warner Books, Inc.

Oken, A. (1973). *As Above, So Below*. New York: Bantam Books, Inc.

Pearce, J. C. (1975). *Exploring the Crack In the Cosmic Egg*. New York: Pocket Books, Simon & Schuster, Inc.

Reps, P. (compiler) (1957). *Zen Flesh, Zen Bones: A Collection of Zen and Pre-Zen Writings*. Tokyo & Rutland, Vt.: Charles E. Tuttle Co.

Ross, N. W. (compiler and editor) (1960). *The World of Zen: An East-West Anthology*. New York: Vintage Books.

Suzuki, D. T. (1960). *Manual of Zen Buddhism*. New York: Grove Press, Inc.

Suzuki, S. (1970). *Zen Mind, Beginner's Mind*. New York: John Weatherhill, Inc.

Swami Prabhavananda and Isherwood, C. (translators) (1951). *The Song of God: Bhagavad-Gita*. New York: Mentor Books.

The Jerusalem Bible (1968). Garden City, NY: Doubleday & Co.

Watts, A. (1975). *Tao: The Watercourse Way*. New York: Pantheon Books.

Biographical Note

Martin Treon was born in St. Paul, Minnesota (USA) on February 11, 1937. Currently he lives in Vermillion, South Dakota, and is on the faculty there at the University of South Dakota in the Communication Disorders Program, Department of Communication.